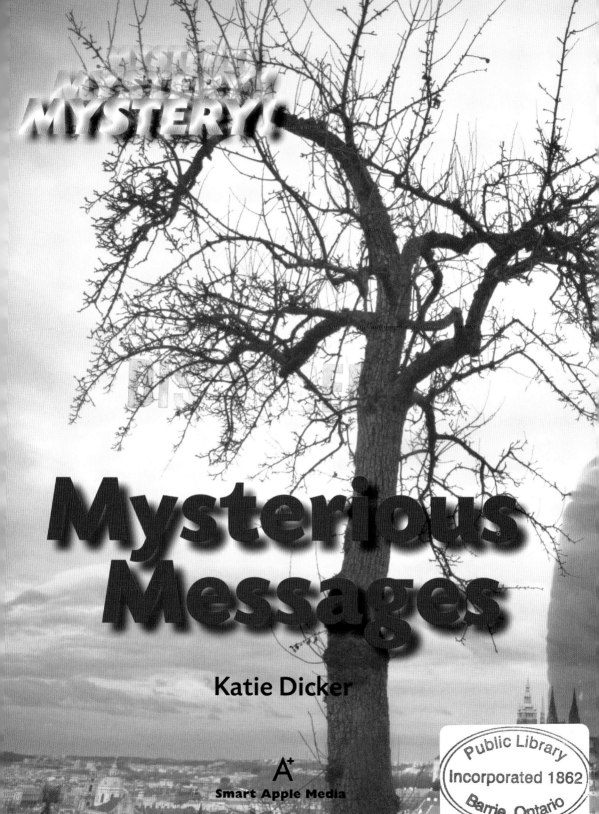

Mysterious Messages

Katie Dicker

A+
Smart Apple Media

Published by Smart Apple Media,
an imprint of Black Rabbit Books
P.O. Box 3263, Mankato, Minnesota, 56002
www.blackrabbitbooks.com

Designed by Hel James
Edited by Mary-Jane Wilkins

Cataloging-in-Publication Data is available from
the Library of Congress

ISBN 978-1-62588-203-5

Photo acknowledgements
title Chalabala/Thinkstock, page 3 Slava Gerj/Shutterstock;
4-5 Chalabala/Thinkstock, 5 Jakez; 7 Aleksey Stemmer/both
Shutterstock; 8 Jupiterimages/Thinkstock; 9 Alastair Wallace;
10 OPIS Zagreb; 11 A. Einsiedler; 12 Michael Rosskothen/
all Shutterstock; 14 Steven Wynn; 15 Comstock Images/
both Thinkstock; 16 justasc/Shutterstock; 19 Alexey Zarodov;
21 Photodisc; 22 Frank Vinken; 24 Chalabala/all Thinkstock
Cover Alvaro German Vilela/Shutterstock

Artwork Q2A Media Art Bank

Printed in China

DAD0054
032014
9 8 7 6 5 4 3 2 1

Contents

Spirit World   4

Solving a Murder   6

Past Lives   8

Sinking Ship   12

Sleep Talk   14

New Life   18

Glossary   22

Web Sites   23

Index   24

Spirit World

What happens when people die? Do they lie in a **grave**, or become part of a **spirit world**? Some people say they've had messages from the spirits of dead people.

Buried Bodies

In 1971, Maria Gomez Pereira saw a mark on her kitchen floor. When she cleaned it, the mark started to look like a human face. Maria's husband changed the floor, but more faces appeared. Eventually, the council dug up the floor. They found skeletons buried underneath—some had their heads missing.

Strange Stories

Animals have been known to predict the future. One day, a woman was driving with her cat in the car. The cat became restless, jumped into the front and bit the woman, forcing her to stop. Just at that moment, a large tree fell on the road, a few yards ahead of them. The cat had saved their lives.

4

Escape from Death

Wolf Messing was a **psychic** who could see into the future. In 1948, he visited the city of Ashgabat in Turkmenistan to put on a show. Wolf sensed something terrible was about to happen, so he canceled his show and left the city. Three days later, a huge earthquake struck. Around 50,000 people were killed.

Some people say they can talk to the spirits of dead people. Others claim they can see into the future.

This statue is a reminder of the earthquake that destroyed the city of Ashgabat in Turkmenistan in 1948.

Solving a Murder

Sometimes, mothers have a feeling that their children are in danger. Ghosts have been known to talk to their parents, too.

Strange Feeling

In the 1890s, Elva Heaster from West Virginia was found dead at her home. When she was buried, Elva's head seemed to wobble as she was lowered into her grave. Her mother was suspicious. She had always felt that there was something evil about Elva's new husband, Erasmus.

A Ghost's Tale

For four nights, Elva's ghost appeared to her mother and told a terrible tale. Erasmus had beaten her, and one day he had strangled her. She said her neck had been "squeezed off."

The Truth Revealed

When this tale was reported, Elva's body was dug up. Her neck was broken, and she had been strangled to death. Erasmus was tried for her murder and put in prison.

Elva was in her grave when she appeared to her mother and recounted her murder.

Past Lives

Some people say they have lived and died before. They claim to have been someone else in a past life!

Curious Tales

In the 1970s, a woman from Wales named Jane Evans said that she could remember six previous lives. When she was **hypnotized**, Jane told a tale of living in England at the time of the Romans, and said she had lived as a nun in Iowa during the 20th century.

Sometimes, people are hypnotized to help them remember past events.

8

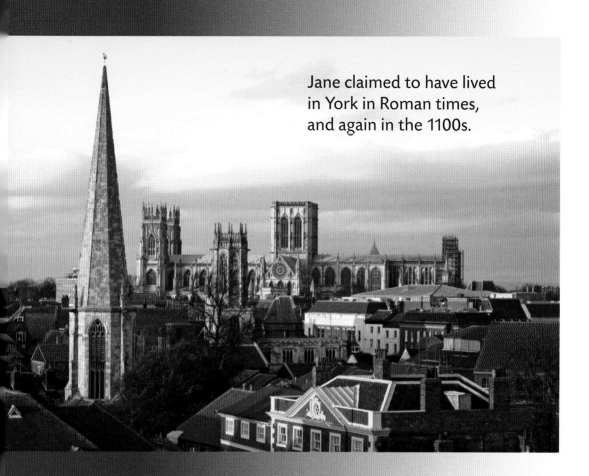
Jane claimed to have lived in York in Roman times, and again in the 1100s.

Hiding Place

Jane also said she had been Rebecca, a Jewish woman living in York, in England, in 1189. When Christians were killing the Jews, Jane and her two children hid in the cellar of a church. They were found and killed. Years later, a historian came across the church where "Rebecca" must have died. He couldn't find a cellar, but six months later, workmen uncovered the hidden cellar.

A Woman's Tale

Swarnlata was born in India in 1948. When she was three, she went traveling with her father. Far from home, Swarnlata recognized a place where she said she had lived as a married woman called Biya, with two sons. When Swarnlata was ten, she discovered Biya's house. She recognized members of her old family and knew facts about their lives. She remembered everything as it had been in 1939, when Biya died.

Swarnlata was born in Pradesh in northern India in 1948.

Childhood Stories

The Indian **sitar** player Ravi Shankar claimed to remember past lives. When he was two, he asked his parents for toys from a house they did not know about. Then, when he was six, he told his parents a terrible tale—two relatives had killed him with a razor. Six months before Ravi was born, a six-year-old boy was killed in this way.

Ravi Shankar had a birthmark that looked like a razor cut around his neck. Was this a sign of one of his past lives?

Buddhist Beliefs

Followers of the Buddhist religion believe when someone dies, their soul is reborn in the body of another person or animal. When the **Dalai Lama** dies, Buddhists say his soul becomes part of the new Dalai Lama. Boys born soon after his death are tested. If a boy recognizes things from the Dalai Lama's life, he becomes the new Buddhist leader.

Sinking Ship

In 1912, the largest passenger ship ever built set sail from Southampton, England, to New York. There were only a few lifeboats on board and *Titanic* was called "unsinkable," but four days into her voyage, disaster struck.

Sixth Sense?

At midnight on April 14, 1912, the ship hit an iceberg and sank. More than 1,500 people died. Some passengers had canceled their trip—including Milton Hershey, owner of the Hershey Chocolate Company, and J. P. Morgan, one of the richest men in the world. Perhaps they had felt uneasy about the ship? Twenty-two engine room workers were late for duty that day and their lives were saved because the *Titanic* sailed without them.

Life at Sea?

Donald Wollam was born in Illinois in 1960. He was terrified of water, but loved stories about the Titanic. He described a girl and boy playing on board. Donald drowned when he was 19. Later, his mother heard a Titanic survivor talking about her time on board, playing with her brother. Had Donald been on the ship in a previous life?

Strange Stories

Morgan Robertson wrote a book about a luxury liner called the *Titan* 14 years before the *Titanic* sank. In his story, the unsinkable ship strikes an iceberg one night in April. There are not enough lifeboats and nearly everyone dies.

Sleep Talk

Many people say they hear messages in their dreams. Some are hard to understand, but others seem perfectly clear. Some dreams even describe events in the future.

Death Warning

In 1865, President Abraham Lincoln told his wife and two staff about a strange dream he had three nights in a row. In the dream, he heard crying in the **White House**. *When he went to investigate, he found his own body lying ready to be buried. He was also told that the president had been killed. About two weeks later, Lincoln was shot dead at Ford's Theater.*

Did President Lincoln see his own death in a dream?

Hidden Treasure

Nearly 3,500 years ago, the Egyptian **pharaoh** Thutmose IV had a dream. A god told him to clear away the sand in a particular area. He said it would reveal a sphinx lost under the sands of Egypt for hundreds of years. Thutmose ordered the sand to be cleared, and the sphinx was found.

This sphinx was buried under sand for centuries, until a dream revealed exactly where it was.

Battle Facts

Soldiers sometimes dream about their death before they are killed. Some dreams show exactly what will happen. Before the battle of Fair Oaks in the Civil War, a soldier dreamed he had only a week to live. He described a battle that would take place in seven days, and said which men would die and where they would be found. The battle took place a week later, just as he described.

Strange Stories

In 1979, David Booth called American Airlines with a warning. He had dreamed that an American Airlines DC-10 plane had crashed among tall buildings. A few days later, an engine fell off a DC-10 flying from Chicago. It crashed into buildings, killing everyone on board.

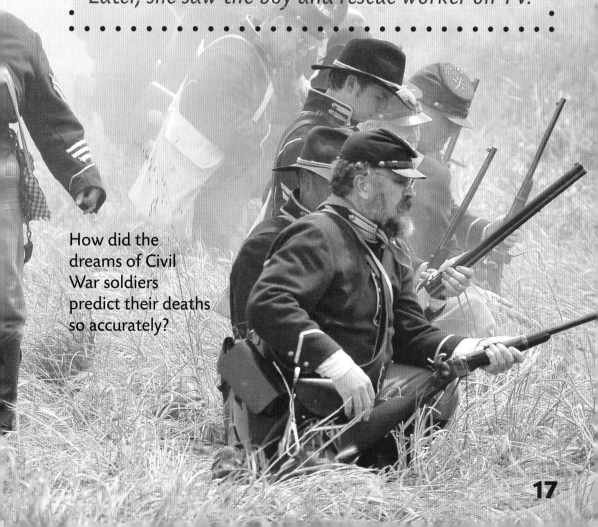

Dreaming of Disaster

In 1966, tragedy struck the Welsh village of Aberfan. A huge mountain of coal waste fell on the village school, killing 116 children. People dreamed about the tragedy before it happened. One woman saw coal pouring down a mountain in a dream; a rescue worker wearing a pointed hat pulled a boy from the wreckage. Later, she saw the boy and rescue worker on TV.

How did the dreams of Civil War soldiers predict their deaths so accurately?

New Life

*When someone has just died, their organs can be used by a patient whose own organs no longer work properly. An **organ transplant** can save someone's life. There are tales of people who seem to take on some of the dead person's personality, too.*

Changed Person

In 1988, Claire Sylvia had a heart and lung transplant that saved her life. But after the operation, she was not quite the same person. She began to like beer, green bell peppers, and chicken nuggets—all things she hadn't liked before. She became more sure of herself, too.

Claire Sylvia's tastes changed after her heart and lung transplant.

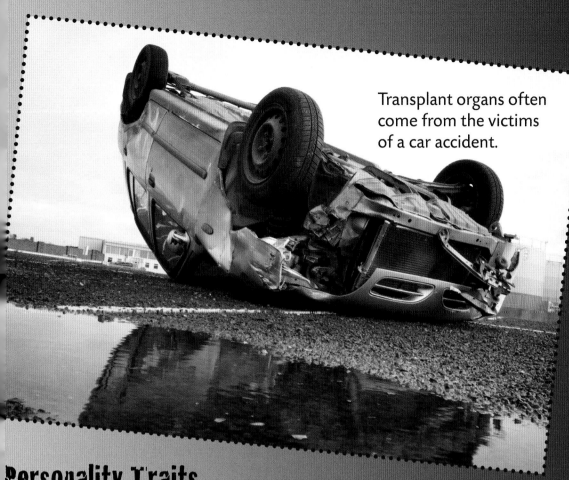

Transplant organs often come from the victims of a car accident.

Personality Traits

In a dream, Claire said she had met a young man called Tim L and seemed to "breathe him into her body." Claire discovered that her organ donor was a young man called Tim Lamirande who had died in a motorcycle accident. His family said he had liked beer, green bell peppers, and chicken nuggets. Perhaps some of Tim's personality had passed into Claire, too?

New Hobbies

In October 2005, Lynda Gammons gave one of her kidneys to her husband Ian, who needed a transplant. Soon after the operation, Ian started to enjoy baking and cleaning the house. He had hated housework before! Though previously a cat lover, Ian also started to like dogs.

Strange Stories

An eight-year-old girl who had a heart transplant helped police to find the man who had murdered her donor. After her transplant, the girl had terrible dreams about a murder. She recalled details of the time and place, the weapon used, and the clothes worn by the murderer. When she reported these facts, the police tracked down the donor's killer and he was **convicted**.

When Lynda donated a kidney to her husband, they began to share similar hobbies.

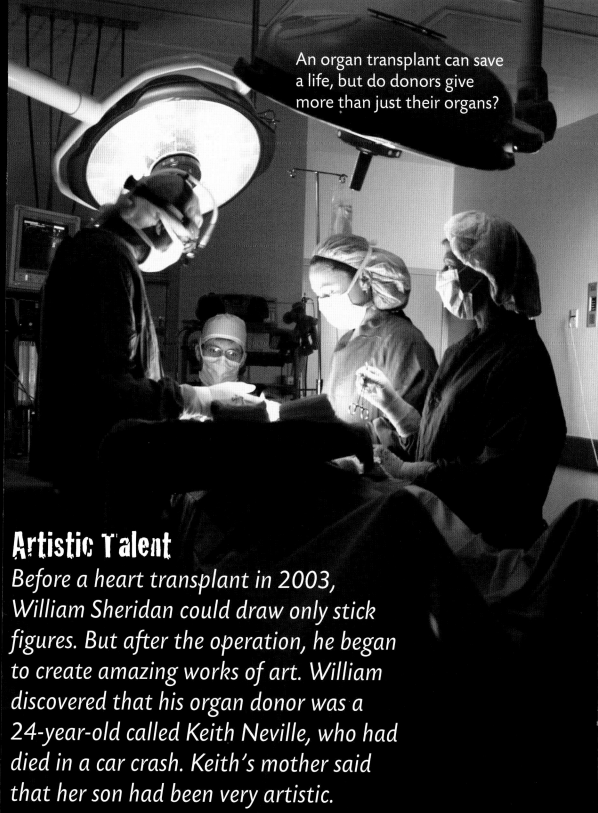

An organ transplant can save a life, but do donors give more than just their organs?

Artistic Talent

Before a heart transplant in 2003, William Sheridan could draw only stick figures. But after the operation, he began to create amazing works of art. William discovered that his organ donor was a 24-year-old called Keith Neville, who had died in a car crash. Keith's mother said that her son had been very artistic.

Glossary

convicted
A person is convicted when he or she is found guilty of committing a crime.

Dalai Lama
The name given to the leader of the Buddhist religion.

grave
A place where a dead body is buried.

hypnotized
When someone is hypnotized they are put into a trance-like state, in which they can hear and answer questions, and may remember past events.

organ transplant
A medical operation that removes an organ from one person and puts it into the body of another person, to replace a damaged organ.

pharaoh
A ruler in ancient Egypt.

22

psychic
A person who is said to read minds, talk
to dead people, or predict the future.

sitar
A stringed instrument, often played in India.

spirit world
An imaginary place where the spirits of dead
people are said to live.

White House
The official home and office of the President
of the United States, in Washington, D.C.

Web Sites

www.scaryforkids.com/true-ghost-stories
Real ghost stories from around the world.

www.ghoststudy.com
Find out more about ghosts and look at some
haunted photographs!

http://paranormal.about.com/od/ghostsandhauntings
All you need to know about ghosts and haunted
places.

Index

American Civil War 16, 17
animals 4, 11, 20

Booth, David 16
buddhists 11

Dalai Lama 11, 22
dreams 14, 15, 16, 17, 19, 20

earthquakes 5
Evans, Jane 8, 9

Gammons, Lynda 20
ghosts 6, 7
graves 4, 6, 7, 22

Heaster, Elva 6, 7
Hershey, Milton 12
hypnotism 8, 9, 22

Lamirande, Tim 19
Lincoln, Abraham 14

Messing, Wolf 5
Morgan, J.P. 12

Neville, Keith 21

organ transplants
  18, 19, 20, 21, 22

Pereira, Maria Gomez 4
psychics 5, 23

Robertson, Morgan 13

Shankar, Ravi 11
Sheridan, William 21
spirits 4, 5, 23
Swarnlata 10
Sylvia, Claire 18, 19

Titanic 12, 13

Wollam, Donald 13